CHEMICAL SECRET

There are two ways of committing a crime. You can do it with your eyes open, or you can do it with your eyes closed. Not many of us intend to do wrong, but almost all of us close our eyes to certain kinds of crime.

But what is a crime? Is it something that the law tells us is wrong, or something that we know in our hearts is wrong? There are many kinds of crime – crimes of greed, of violence, of anger and hate. But there are also less obvious crimes – the ones that we commit against the world: against the sky, the sea, the land. They are the crimes that we commit against the future and against our children – by closing our eyes and pretending that we cannot see.

John Duncan is a biologist. When he took the job at the chemical factory, he thought he was protecting his children. He wanted to buy them the good things of life: a big house, a boat, exciting holidays . . . But what kind of future was he buying them?

OXFORD BOOKWORMS LIBRARY
Thriller & Adventure

Chemical Secret

Stage 3 (1000 headwords)

.

Series Editor: Jennifer Bassett
Founder Editor: Tricia Hedge
Activities Editors: Jennifer Bassett and Alison Baxter

TIM VICARY

Chemical Secret

OXFORD UNIVERSITY PRESS

OXFORD

UNIVERSITY PRESS

Great Clarendon Street, Oxford OX2 6DP

Oxford University Press is a department of the University of Oxford.
It furthers the University's objective of excellence in research, scholarship,
and education by publishing worldwide in

Oxford New York

Auckland Cape Town Dar es Salaam Hong Kong Karachi
Kuala Lumpur Madrid Melbourne Mexico City Nairobi
New Delhi Shanghai Taipei Toronto

With offices in

Argentina Austria Brazil Chile Czech Republic France Greece
Guatemala Hungary Italy Japan Poland Portugal Singapore
South Korea Switzerland Thailand Turkey Ukraine Vietnam

OXFORD and OXFORD ENGLISH are registered trade marks of
Oxford University Press in the UK and in certain other countries

ISBN 978 0 19 479112 0

A complete recording of this Bookworms edition of
Chemical Secret is available on audio CD ISBN 978 0 19 479093 2

Printed in Hong Kong

ACKNOWLEDGEMENTS
Illustrated by: Chris Koelle

Word count (main text): 10,150 words

For more information on the Oxford Bookworms Library,
visit www.oup.com/bookworms

CONTENTS

1

A new start

'Mr Duncan? Come in please. Mr Wilson will see you now.'

'Thank you.' John Duncan stood up and walked nervously towards the door. He was a tall, thin man, about forty-five years old, in an old grey suit. It was his best suit, but it was ten years old now. He had grey hair and glasses. His face looked sad and tired.

Inside the room, a man stood up to welcome him. 'Mr Duncan? Pleased to meet you. My name's David Wilson. This is one of our chemists, Mary Carter.'

John Duncan shook hands with both of them, and sat down. It was a big office, with a thick carpet on the floor and beautiful pictures on the walls. David Wilson was a young man, in an expensive black suit. He had a big gold ring on one finger. He smiled at John.

'I asked Miss Carter to come because she's one of our best chemists. She discovered our wonderful new paint, in fact. When . . . I mean, if you come to work here, you will work with her.'

'Oh, I see.' John looked at Mary. She was older than Wilson – about thirty-five, perhaps – with short brown hair, and a pretty, friendly face. She was wearing a white coat with a lot of pens in the top pocket. She smiled at him kindly, but John felt miserable.

I'll never get this job, he thought. I'm too old! Employers want younger people these days.

'Mr Duncan? Pleased to meet you,' said David Wilson.

David Wilson was looking at some papers. 'Now, Mr Duncan,' he said, 'I see that you are a very good biologist. You worked at a university . . . and then for two very famous companies. But . . . you stopped working as a biologist nine years ago. Why was that?'

'I've always had two interests in my life,' John said, 'biology and boats. My wife was a famous sailor . . . Rachel Horsley . . . Perhaps you remember her. She sailed around the world alone in a small boat.'

'Yes,' said David Wilson, 'I remember her.'

'So we started a business,' said John. 'We made small boats together, and sold them.'

'And did the business go well?' asked Wilson.

'Very well at first. Then we wanted to build bigger, better boats. We borrowed too much money. And then my wife . . .' John stopped speaking.

'Yes, the Sevens Race. I remember now,' said David Wilson.

Both men were silent for a moment. Wilson remembered the newspaper reports of the storm and the lives lost at sea. He looked at the man who sat sadly in front of him.

'So, after my wife died,' continued John, 'I closed the business. That was five years ago.'

'I see,' said David Wilson. 'It's a hard world, the world of business.' He looked at John's old grey suit. 'So now you want a job as a biologist. Well, this is a chemical company, Mr Duncan. We make paint. But we need a biologist to make sure that everything in this factory is safe. We want someone to tell the government that it's safe to work here, and that it's safe to have a paint factory near the town. That's important to us.'

'And if something's not safe, then of course we'll change it,' Mary Carter said. David Wilson looked at her, but he didn't say anything.

'Yes, I see,' John began nervously. 'Well, I think I could do that. I mean, when I worked for Harper Chemicals in London I . . .' He talked for two or three minutes about his work. David Wilson listened, but he didn't say anything. Then he smiled. It was a cold, hard smile, and it made John feel uncomfortable. He remembered his old suit and grey hair, and he wished he hadn't come.

'You really need this job, don't you, Mr Duncan?' David Wilson said. 'You need it a lot.'

'Yes, I do,' he said quietly. But he thought: I hate you, Wilson. You're enjoying this. You like making people feel small. I hate people like you.

Wilson's smile grew bigger. He stood up, and held out his hand. 'OK,' he said. 'When can you start?'

'What?' John was very surprised. 'What did you say?'

'I said, "When can you start?", Mr Duncan. We need you in our factory as soon as possible. Will Monday be OK?'

'You mean I've got the job?'

'Of course. Congratulations!' Wilson shook John's hand. 'My secretary will tell you about your pay. You'll have your own office, and a company car, of course. I'd like you to start work with Mary on Monday. Is that OK?'

'I . . . Yes, yes, of course. That's fine. Thank you, thank you very much.'

2

At home

'Hi, Dad. Your supper's in the kitchen.'

John's sixteen-year-old daughter, Christine, was sitting at the table doing her homework. His son Andrew, who was thirteen, was watching television.

'Thanks, Christine,' John said. 'I'm sorry I'm late. Is everything OK?'

'Fine, thanks.' Christine gave him a quick smile, then continued with her work. John got his food from the kitchen. Fried fish and chips. The food was dry and didn't taste very good. But he didn't say anything about that. John was not a good cook himself and his children were no better. His wife had been a good cook, he remembered.

John tried to eat the terrible supper and looked around the small, miserable flat. The furniture was twenty years old, the wallpaper and carpets were cheap and dirty. The rooms were all small, and he could see no trees or gardens from the windows – just the lights from hundreds of other flats. And there were books, clothes, and newspapers on the floor.

Once, when his wife had been alive, he had had a fine house. A beautiful big house in the country, with a large garden. They had had lots of new furniture, two cars, expensive holidays – everything they needed. He had had a good job; they hadn't needed to think about money. And then he had started the boat-building company, and his luck had ended.

John looked around the small, miserable flat.

When Rachel had died, John had been terribly un-happy – much too unhappy to think about business. A few months later his company had closed, and he had lost all his money. John had had to sell his beautiful house in the country, and move to this miserable flat.

And for the last two years, he hadn't had a job at all. He was a poor man, and an unlucky one, too. He had tried for lots of jobs, and got none of them. There were too many bright young biologists. But now that was all going to change. He looked at his daughter and smiled.

'Did you have a good day at school, Christine?' he asked her.

'Oh, all right, I suppose,' she said. She didn't look very happy. 'I've got a letter for you.'

She pushed the letter across the table, and he opened it. It was from her school. One of the teachers was taking the children on a skiing holiday to the mountains in Switzerland. It cost £400 for ten days. Parents who wanted their children to go had to send the money to the school before February 25th.

John's smile grew bigger. 'Do you want to go on this holiday, Christine?' he asked.

She looked at him strangely. 'Of course I do, Dad,' she said. 'But I can't, can I? We haven't got £400.'

'No, I suppose not.' He looked at her carefully through his thick glasses. She was a clever, strong girl – good at her schoolwork, good at sports. But she had never been skiing; John hadn't had enough money.

'Are your friends going?' he asked her.

'Some of them, yes. Miranda, Jane, Nigel – the rich

ones, you know. But they often go skiing; it's easy for them. I know I can't go, Dad. Throw the letter away.'

John looked at her, and felt his heart beating quickly. 'No, don't do that, Christine,' he said. 'Perhaps you can go, if you want to. Why not?'

Christine laughed. 'What's happened, Dad? Have you robbed a bank or something?'

John stood up. He went into the kitchen and got himself a drink. 'No,' he said, when he came back. 'But something interesting happened today. Put your homework away, Christine – and turn that TV off, Andrew. I've got something to tell you.'

'Oh, not now, Dad!' said Andrew. 'This is an exciting story.'

John smiled. 'I've got an exciting story, too, Andrew. Come and listen.'

John Duncan's children lived in an old, untidy flat, they had no money, and they often ate awful food. But they could still talk to their father. So Andrew turned off the TV, and sat down in a big armchair beside his father and Christine.

The story didn't sound very exciting at first. 'I went to a factory today,' John said. 'That paint factory by the river. No, wait, Andrew. Paint factories can be very exciting. They gave me a job there. I'm going to have my own office, a big car, lots of money – in fact, we're going to be rich . . .!'

'*We're going to be rich . . .!*'

3

Rich man

John Duncan started work on Monday, and Mary Carter showed him round the factory. The most important thing that the company produced was a new paint for cars. It was a very strong, hard paint, which nothing could damage. Mary and her chemists had developed it, and they had tested it all over the world. Neither acid nor salt water could damage it, and cars came back from both the Arctic and the Sahara looking like new.

The company was beginning to make a lot of money from this paint, and it had brought four hundred new jobs to the town.

One day, when he was working with the paint, John spilt some of the waste products on his leg. He cleaned it off quickly, but it left a red, painful place on his skin, which would not go away. It kept him awake at night. He told his doctor what he had spilt on it, and the doctor looked at him strangely.

'So these chemicals had something to do with the new paint, did they?' the doctor asked carefully.

'Yes, I told you. It was a bottle of the waste products. I was looking at them in my office.'

'I see.' The doctor looked out of the window thoughtfully. His fingers moved quietly on his desk. 'And your company is producing a lot of these waste products now, I suppose.'

'Yes, of course.' John was in a hurry. He had to meet

someone important in ten minutes. 'Look, can you give me something to put on it, or not?'

'Oh yes.' The doctor began to write something on a piece of paper. 'Put this on night and morning, and the pain will go in a day or two. But I'm afraid the skin there will stay red for a year or two. They're nasty chemicals, Mr Duncan, you know.'

'Yes, I know.' John smiled at him. 'But don't worry, Doctor, we're very careful with them in the factory. No one can go near them without special safe clothing. You can come and see if you like.'

'I'm very pleased to hear it,' said the doctor. He gave the piece of paper to John.

'Thank you,' said John. He went towards the door.

'Mr Duncan?'

'Yes?' John looked back, surprised.

'Where do these waste products go, when the factory has finished with them? Into the river?'

'Well, yes, of course,' said John. 'But it's all right, you know,' he added quickly. 'It's very carefully checked, all the time. It's a big river, and we only produce a few hundred litres of the waste products a day. And we're only two kilometres from the sea, after all.'

'Good,' said the doctor. 'I wouldn't want anyone to drink those waste products, that's all.'

'They won't, Doctor,' said John. 'All the drinking water comes out of the river five kilometres upstream, you know that. Who's going to drink salt water from the river mouth, for heaven's sake? Chemists from London have checked it, too, you know, and our company lawyers

'So these chemicals had something to do with
the new paint, did they?' the doctor asked.

know all about it. So it's not dangerous and we're not doing anything wrong. Don't worry about it.'

He went out of the door, and after half an hour he had forgotten the conversation.

He was a very busy man now. All day he had to test different types of paints, and make sure they were safe. He was also busy buying a big, comfortable house for his family, with a large field beside it, where Christine could keep a horse. The house was half a kilometre from the sea, and its gardens went down to the river. There was an empty boathouse there.

'Can we have a boat, Dad?' Andrew asked. 'I mean, not now, of course, but one day – when you've finished paying for the house, perhaps?'

John laughed. His children had been poor for so long. But now he could buy them anything they wanted.

'You can have a boat now, if you want, my son,' he said happily. 'If I can afford a big house like this, I can certainly afford a small boat. We'll go fishing every week, shall we? And I'll teach you both to sail in the evenings. I've always wanted to do that, you know.'

He could not believe how lucky he was. He had a good job at last, a fine home, and his children had everything they wanted. He only wished his wife, Rachel, was alive to enjoy it with him. There was only one thing that he could not give his children now. He could not give them back their mother.

*It was a big, comfortable house, and its gardens
went down to the river.*

The seals

A few months later, John invited Mary to a meal in the new house. It was a difficult evening. He had never invited anyone to their old flat, and the children's friends never came for meals. The new house was very untidy, and John was nervous about the food. He and Christine cooked a chicken because they thought it was easy. But the chicken was tasteless and the rice was too soft.

Mary smiled, and pretended not to notice. But the evening went badly. Christine was angry with her because she tidied up the kitchen, and Andrew was angry with her because she didn't want to watch TV. Both the children went to bed early, and thought about their mother.

But Mary came again, on a Sunday, and John took them all out in their new boat. That was much better. Mary didn't know how to sail, so the children had to tell her what to do. She did what she was told, and seemed to be happy. John sat at the back of the boat, and watched his children quietly. He felt proud of them, and he thought they were proud of him too. The first time Mary and the children laughed together, John felt a big smile come onto his face.

It was a beautiful, sunny day in the middle of May. There was a good wind, and the sailing was fun. The boat sailed fast, over small, white-topped waves. The sky was blue and clear. They sailed down to the mouth of the river, where there were lots of small islands and sand-banks.

'Look, Dad, quick! Over there! What are they?' Andrew pointed excitedly to one of the long, low sandbanks.

'Seals,' said John. 'Haven't you seen them before?'

'No,' said Andrew. 'Only in films. Not in real life.' His face was shining, excited, happy. 'Do they really live here?'

'Yes. It's a group of seal families. The mothers come here every year to have their babies.'

They sailed closer to the sandbank, until they were only about twenty metres away from the seals. Wet, shiny seal mothers lifted their heads and looked at them with their blue eyes. The baby seals were drinking milk from their mothers, climbing over them, and playing in the shallow water. Then a big father seal lifted his head and stared angrily at them.

'I think they're beautiful,' said Mary. 'I never knew they lived here, so close to the town. It makes me feel really happy, just to see them.'

'Yes, it does, doesn't it?' said Christine. 'I think nothing can be really wrong with the world, if they can live here, all by themselves, with no one looking after them.'

'Yes,' said Mary. 'And they're really beautiful, too. Look! Did you see that little one, playing on his mother's back? I wish I could do that!'

John smiled, as he watched Mary and his children laughing and talking together. He thought the world was a good place, too.

"It's a group of seal families,' John said. 'The mothers come here every year to have their babies.'

The new experiment

A few days later, John asked Mary to look at another experiment. He took her into a long, quiet room at the back of the factory. The room was full of the noises of small animals.

'I've been testing the waste products,' he said. 'Here, look at this.' He gave her a sheet of paper. 'Some of these rats have had the waste products in their food and drinking water. There's no real problem yet. One or two have become ill, but not many. There's nothing very serious.'

Mary read the results carefully. She didn't like this kind of experiment, but she knew it was necessary. And John was right; no rats had died, and not very many were ill.

'So what do you want to show me?' she asked.

'This,' he said. He opened a box by the window. 'These ten rats have had the waste products in their drinking water for two weeks now. I gave them a lot – five parts per million. They're going to have babies today. If the babies are OK, we've got nothing to worry about.'

'Oh, John,' she said. 'What an awful thing to do!'

'I know, I know,' he said. But he wasn't listening. 'Look,' he said excitedly. 'Some of them have been born already!'

He lifted some of the baby rats out of the box and looked at them through a magnifying glass.

'Oh dear,' he said at last, sadly. 'Perhaps there is a problem. Look!'

Mary looked through the magnifying glass. She began to feel ill. There was a long silence.

'There certainly is a problem!' Mary's voice sounded loud and high in the quiet room. She stared at the small animals under the magnifying glass. 'Baby rats with no eyes, no ears, six legs! Oh John! John! What have you done?'

He looked at her strangely. 'It's awful, isn't it? But I had to know. And remember, Mary – their mothers have had five parts per million of these chemicals in their drinking water for two weeks. That's a lot – much, much more than we're putting in the river.'

Mary looked away from the rats. She remembered the beautiful afternoon that they had spent with John's children, sailing on the clear blue water. 'John, these waste products are dangerous!' she said. 'We've got to stop putting them in the river!'

'Of course, of course.' John put his hand on her arm, to comfort her. But it was the same hand – the hand that had held the rats. 'Of course we'll stop it, if we need to, Mary. The company can build machines to clean the waste products. I'll start my report for David Wilson next week.'

'But . . .' She turned round to face him. His hand fell from her arm. 'Don't you think we should stop making the paint now, John? Perhaps it'll take years to build those machines, and we're putting the chemicals into the river right now!'

A shadow crossed his face. His eyes looked at hers, then away, out of the window.

'I . . . don't think we need to do that now, Mary. We're putting very little into the river at the moment. And the

'These waste products are dangerous!' said Mary. 'We've got to stop putting them in the river!'

company will build those machines, won't they?'

She remembered her long years of work, the hundreds of unsuccessful experiments. She touched his hand, and smiled. 'I hope so, John,' she said. 'I really hope so.'

She turned, and went quickly out of the room.

6

The report

John's report took longer than he had thought. It was nearly six weeks later when he went to discuss the results with David Wilson.

Mr Wilson wasn't a scientist. He was a businessman. He knew how to run a business, how to make money.

'Thanks for coming, John.' David Wilson came out from behind his desk and shook hands with John. They sat in two big, comfortable armchairs by the window.

David Wilson's office was large, with a thick carpet and beautiful pictures on the walls. From the window, John could see the river, and the woods and fields on the other side. He felt comfortable, happy, safe.

'I've read your report,' Wilson began. Then he stopped, and lit a cigarette. 'Not very good, is it?'

'What?' John stared at him in surprise.

Wilson smiled, and moved his hand through the clouds of smoke. 'No, no, don't worry – I don't mean the report is bad, of course not. You've worked very hard, and done your job well. What I mean is, I don't like the ideas at the end of the report.'

'What's wrong with them?'

'They're too expensive.' The two men stared at each other for a moment, and John felt cold and sick in his stomach. Wilson smiled, but it wasn't the kind of smile that John liked.

'Look, John,' he said. 'Your report says that we should build some new machines to clean up the waste products before they go into the river, right? And those machines will cost *two million pounds!* Where do you think we can find all that? Money doesn't grow on trees, you know!'

'No, of course not.' John's mouth was dry. He took a drink of water, and felt his hand shaking. 'But we're selling a lot of the new paint. We're making millions of pounds every month from that, aren't we?'

'We're doing very well, yes,' said Wilson. 'But if we spend two million pounds to build these new machines, the paint will have to cost more, and we won't sell so much.'

'But – we've got to do it,' said John. 'These waste products are much more dangerous than I'd thought. Didn't you read that in my report? When I put the chemicals in rats' drinking water, some of the baby rats were born without eyes and ears. One didn't have any legs, and one had six.' He shivered. 'And some were born without legs when they drank only two parts per million. We can't put those chemicals in the river.'

'Of course I read that, John. I read your report very carefully indeed. And your report also says that on most days we put less than two parts per million into the river. No, wait, listen to me for a minute! We both know that

'Where do you think we can find two million pounds?' Wilson said.

no drinking water comes out of this part of the river, don't we? And in two kilometres the river goes out into the sea. So why is it dangerous? Nobody is ever going to drink it, John! We don't need to build these new machines!'

John thought of his children, sailing on the river in their boat. He thought of the seals, and people fishing, and little children playing on the beach and swimming. 'We've got to build them!' he said.

David Wilson looked at him carefully. His voice, when he spoke, was very quiet and hard. 'Listen to me, John. You're a very good scientist, and we're lucky to have you in this company. But you're not a businessman, and I am. Look at this.' He picked up a sheet of paper, and held it across the table for John to see. It showed how much money the company had. 'We borrowed ten million pounds last year, and we employed four hundred more people. Think how much that means to a small town like this!'

'I know,' said John. 'But . . .'

'Just a minute. Listen to me. If we build these cleaning machines of yours, people will lose their jobs – a lot of people! This company can't afford to borrow any more money, John. We just can't do it!'

John stood up. 'And what happens if people get ill because of this? Have you thought of that? What will the newspapers say then?'

'No one will get ill, because no one drinks that water, John. The newspapers will never know about it.'

'They will if I tell them.'

There was a long silence. Then David Wilson stood up. He walked past John Duncan, without looking at him, and sat down behind his desk. When he looked up, his eyes were cold and grey, like stones from the beach.

'If you do that, John, I shall say you're a liar. You'll lose your job. You'll have to sell your house, and go back to living in a nasty little flat. You'll never get another job, and you'll never have a house or any money again. You'll just be an old man, walking the streets without friends or money. Is that what you want?'

John didn't answer. He stood for a long time, and stared at David Wilson, and didn't say a word. After nearly two minutes, Wilson smiled – a thin quiet smile.

'But if you stay with us, you will be paid twice as much next year. And no one will ever be hurt, because no one will ever drink that water.'

He got up from his desk, came round to the front, and held out his hand. John stood still for a long moment. Then he shook hands.

'Think about it, John,' said David Wilson.

John Duncan turned, and walked slowly towards the door.

7

Christine and Simon

Mary talked to Mr Wilson too, but it was no good. She came out looking tired and very sad.

For many months she argued with David Wilson about

the danger of the waste products, but he would not listen to her. And so, eighteen months after John's report, Mary decided to move to another company. She was pleased, because it was a more important job, but that wasn't the reason she was going. She knew that the cleaning machines would never be built.

John was sad to see her go. He had enjoyed working with her, and she had come to his house several times over the last year and a half. His children liked her now. They had never been so friendly with any woman, since their mother had died.

On her last day, Mary and John had lunch in the factory restaurant together.

'You don't have to go, you know, Mary,' John said. 'This company is very successful, and it's growing all the time. Your new paint has meant four hundred new jobs – all because of your discovery! This isn't a poor town any more – it's becoming successful, rich! People will want to move here from other places.'

He talked about the new sports centre at Andrew's school, which was built with money from the paint company. There were two big, new shops in the town as well, and a new theatre, and a lot of new houses. 'And it's all because of you,' he said. 'It's wonderful, Mary, don't you think?' He smiled at her across the table, and took her hand in his.

She looked at him quietly. He had changed a lot since he had first started working at the factory. For the first six months after he had got the job, he had been really happy and lively. She had always known where he was in the factory, because he was always laughing, or singing to himself.

But for the last eighteen months he had been much quieter. He was always busy, but he didn't sing or laugh, and he didn't often look Mary in the eyes. And when he was alone, he looked tired and sad.

She took her hand away from his, gently. 'You know why I'm going, John,' she said. 'I know what's going into the river, and I don't like to think about it. You should leave, too, and get a job in another company.'

'I'm too old.' John stared at her angrily. 'It isn't easy for me to get a new job. And Mary, the company has been making the paint for more than two years now, and no one's been hurt, have they?'

Mary didn't answer for a moment. Then she said, 'Only you.'

'What do you mean, only me?'

She looked at him sadly. His head was bald now, and he was beginning to look like an old man. Once, she had wanted to marry him. Now, she was pleased that he hadn't asked her.

'Oh, I just meant your leg, of course.' John still had a painful red place on his leg, and sometimes he walked badly because of it. But that wasn't what Mary meant.

John smiled. 'My leg's nearly better. I'd almost forgotten about it. But Mary, before you go . . . I wonder if you could help me. It's a family matter.'

'I see. Well, how can I help? I don't know your children very well, you know.'

'No, of course not. But you're a woman, and . . . well,

'I'm too old. It isn't easy for me to get a new job,'
said John angrily.

it's sometimes difficult for me, as a father on my own. Christine's a young woman now, and she hasn't got a mother to discuss things with. I don't always know what to say.'

'No.' Mary looked at him sadly. She often wondered why he didn't ask her to his house more often. She liked him and his children, and she thought he liked her. 'How old is Christine now?'

'Eighteen. And she wants to get married.'

'Already? She's rather young, isn't she?'

John looked unhappy. 'Well, that's what I say. But she gets so angry with me, Mary, really angry.'

'Who's the young man?'

'He's called Simon MacDonald. He's a journalist – he works for the local newspaper. He's a nice young man, I suppose. But every time I speak to him, we argue. And then Christine always agrees with him, and I get angry with her, too. I don't want to, Mary, but I do. I feel I'm losing her, you see.'

'What do you argue about?'

'Oh, I don't know. Stupid things, really. He belongs to one of these environmental groups – Greenworld, I think – and he's always talking about it. He thinks only young people are right, and everyone over twenty-five is always wrong!'

Mary looked at John thoughtfully.

'Well, what do you want me to do, John? I'm not a mother and I've never been married.'

'No, but . . . you could talk to Christine, perhaps? If you came to our house for Sunday lunch . . .?'

So Mary went to John's house. Simon was there too. They had a meal and talked about horses and sailing. Everyone was polite, and there were no arguments. Later, Mary went with Christine to look at her horse, and Simon stayed with John. In the field, Mary began to talk about Simon.

'He's a fine young man, Christine. He's very clever and kind. He makes me think of your father.'

'My father! He's nothing like my father! And Dad hates him!'

'I'm sure he doesn't.'

'He does! He says he's too old for me, and I mustn't see him! He thinks I'm still a little girl, Mary! But I'm eighteen! I want to get married!'

'Tell me more about Simon . . .'

And so for a long time Mary stood in the quiet, lonely field. She helped Christine give food to her horse, and listened to her talk about Simon. Simon, Christine said, was kind, intelligent, very hard-working. He liked sailing and riding, and he wanted to make the world a cleaner, better place. He made her feel important, like an adult, not a child any more. She had met his parents, and they liked her a lot. It was only her father . . .

'So what should I do, Mary?' Christine asked.

Mary put her hand on the horse's neck. 'I'm not sure,' she said. 'I think you should marry him, but you don't want to make your father angry, do you? That's not the best way to start your life with Simon.'

'No, but I will if I have to!'

'Would you like me to talk to him? Perhaps he'll listen

'I'm eighteen! I want to get married?' said Christine.

to me. It's difficult for him – you're his only daughter, and he's probably very worried about it.'

'Oh, would you, Mary? Please. I want Dad to like Simon, really, but he's always nasty to him.'

'I'll do my best, my dear, but I don't know if it'll work.'

Mary did try, very hard, before she moved to Scotland for her new job. She spoke to John on the phone, and sometimes they had a cup of coffee together in town. She was surprised how carefully John listened to her, and how grateful he seemed for her help. He's really a very lonely man, she thought. It must be hard for him with two children and no wife. He used to talk to his children a lot, but he doesn't now.

At last John agreed to the marriage. Mary was invited to a special supper because of the good news. Christine was very happy. She kissed Mary when she arrived, and gave her a small, secret present to thank her. It was a pair of pretty ear-rings. At the meal, John seemed a little nervous, but happy too. He tried hard to smile, and thanked Mary, although he didn't think of giving her a present. He watched Christine all through the meal. He seemed to be afraid that he would never see her again, and he was very happy when she smiled at him.

Then Simon stood up to say something.

'Mr Duncan,' he said. 'I'll always remember this night. I know how much you love your daughter, and believe me, sir, I love her too. You've been worried about me because you want her to have the best husband possible, and I – well, I can't promise anything, but I'm going to try to be that man. You're a rich man, Mr Duncan, and of

'I'll always remember this night,' said Simon.

course, Christine and I won't have a lot of money at first, but I hope we'll manage.' He smiled at Christine. 'And yesterday, Mr Duncan, I spoke to my employer, and he's going to pay me a little more than before!'

John looked surprised. 'Oh really? Why is that?'

'Well, because he's given me a new job. He's asked me to write about the environment for our newspaper. I have to write a full-page article every week on the environment. And this is the first one. Look here!'

He pulled a page of newspaper out of his pocket, and held it up in front of them. There were pictures of water, sandbanks, and some seals. The headline read:

SEALS AT RIVER MOUTH
HAVE STRANGE DISEASE
Four baby seals found dead

8

The wedding day

The disease among the seals got worse. Three more baby seals died, and one was born without a tail. Scientists came from London to look at them, and there were long articles in the newspapers, but no one was sure what the reasons were. Some people said that it was a disease that was always in the water; some people said the seals were eating diseased fish; and some people said that it was the paint factory near the river.

There was a sewage works near the river too. The sewage from another small town came to it. One day, in the factory, John Duncan found two young chemists testing samples of water from the river. The water came from two kilometres upstream, near the sewage works.

'Why are you doing that?' he asked, surprised.

'It's a special experiment,' one of them answered. 'David Wilson asked us to do it himself. Didn't he tell you, sir?'

John didn't answer. He watched them quietly for several minutes. 'What are the results?' he asked.

'They're bad, sir,' said the young man. But he didn't look worried; he looked pleased, proud of himself. 'That sewage works is putting a lot of nasty things into the river, you know. I think the newspapers will be very interested.'

'The newspapers?' John asked. The young man smiled.

'Yes, Mr Duncan, of course. Our company cares about the environment, doesn't it? That's why we're doing this. We want to help those poor seals, if we can.'

As John walked away, he listened for the sound of quiet laughter behind him. But he heard nothing. Perhaps the young man really believed what he said.

Christine and Simon were married on a fine day in June. When they came back from the church, they had a party in the garden at John's house. Everyone seemed very happy. John liked Simon's parents, and talked to them a lot.

'You're very lucky, Mr Duncan,' Simon's father said. 'You have a beautiful house with a lovely river at the end of the garden.'

Christine and Simon were married on a fine day in June.

'I haven't always been lucky,' John answered. 'People used to say I was a very unlucky man.' He stood still, thinking. He remembered how unhappy he had been in the little flat in the middle of the town. He had been unemployed then, with no money to buy good things for his children. But he had always been able to talk to them. Now he was a rich man, a success, and his children didn't want to talk to him.

He smiled at Mr and Mrs MacDonald. 'Yes,' he said. 'I'm a very lucky man. I have Simon for my son-in-law. I'm very pleased for my daughter.'

Mrs MacDonald was pleased. 'We're very pleased to have Christine for our daughter-in-law, too,' she said. 'And I'm sure Simon will help you with this river, Mr Duncan. I understand there's a disease in it, which is making the seals ill. Simon told me he's going to work very hard to find the reason for that, and clean up the river. I'm sure you're pleased about that, Mr Duncan.'

'Yes, of course.' John had seen Simon's article in the newspaper last night, about the diseases that came from the sewage works. David Wilson had shown it to him. John didn't want to talk about it.

He saw his daughter laughing with Simon, Andrew and some friends. He had never seen her look so happy. He remembered his own wedding, and the hopes he and Rachel had had.

'Let me get you another drink, Mrs MacDonald,' he said. 'We must drink to our children's future, and wish them luck.'

At the bar in the house he met Mary. She came back to

the town sometimes, and twice he had visited her in Scotland.

'This day's been a great success, John,' she said. 'You must be a happy man.'

He touched her arm thoughtfully. 'I'd like to be, Mary,' he said. 'I've tried, you know. I've done my best. But it's their world now. They must do what they can with it.'

9

I don't believe you

'It's not true, Christine. Simon's information is wrong.'

'I don't believe you, Father.'

John and Christine stared at each other angrily. It was a miserable, frightening moment for them both. It was a night three months after the wedding, and Christine had come with some happy news. She had come to tell her father that she was going to have a baby – his first grandchild! For a while they had talked about that, but then Christine had begun to talk about Simon's new job. Simon had found some information about the waste products from the paint factory. His information was dangerous for the company. Simon had written an article in the newspaper, saying that waste products from the paint factory could be killing the baby seals. David Wilson had written to the newspaper immediately, saying that Simon's article was completely untrue.

And so instead of talking happily about the baby,

Christine and her father had argued all evening. John had known for a long time that they would have this argument. And next week in the town there would be a Public Enquiry, when government officials would try to discover the truth. Scientists and lawyers would speak on both sides of the argument. Everyone in the town was talking about the Enquiry – and about Simon's newspaper article.

'Why did David Wilson write to the paper, Father?' Christine asked. 'He's not a scientist, he's just a business-man. Why didn't you write to the paper?'

'I *have* written to the paper,' said John, sadly. 'You'll probably read my letter tomorrow.'

'Oh. What did you say?' Christine asked.

John felt sad. He hadn't wanted to write the letter. He and David Wilson had had a big argument about it. But in the end he had agreed. He had agreed to hide many bad things before, so one more didn't make any difference.

'I said that our waste products don't make the river water dangerous. We've tested them very carefully for many years, and if they are diluted in water, they are not danger-ous at all. There are usually only one and a half parts per million in the river water, that's all. And the seals aren't in the river. They're out at sea. I wrote that in my letter, and I'll say the same thing at the Enquiry next week.'

Christine was watching him carefully as he spoke. She saw how tired and sad his face was. He was looking at his hands most of the time, not at her.

'Father, I want to believe you. But I can't,' she said softly.

He looked up. 'Don't then!' he said angrily. 'You believe Simon, if you want to! He's a journalist, after all – I'm only a biologist, and your father. Why should you believe me?' He stood up angrily, walked to the door, and opened it. 'I'm sorry, Christine. I've had a hard day, I'm tired, and I don't want to sit here listening to my daughter telling me I'm a liar. Go home to Simon. I'm going to bed!'

She got up slowly. 'It's important, Father,' she said slowly. 'It's important for everyone.'

'I know it is, Christine. But the paint factory's important too. It's given a lot to you, and me, and to the people of this town. Try to remember that, and forget about the seals for a while, can't you?'

'There are more important things than money, Father.'

'Are there? You tell that to all the people who work in the company, and live in this town. What are they going to live on, when the factory's closed because of Simon's stupid articles? Can they give their children photographs of baby seals to eat?'

Christine looked at him for a long moment before she went out of the door. 'And what about children who play by the river, Father? What if they drink the river water? What then?'

'Nobody drinks water from that part of the river,' he said. 'And I've told you it isn't dangerous to children.'

Christine closed the door quietly behind her.

10

Greenworld

Two days later Christine and Simon arrived at John's house. It was very early – five o'clock in the morning – and they didn't knock at the door, or try to wake anyone up. In fact John wasn't there; Christine knew he had gone to Scotland to see Mary. He was coming back on the morning of the Enquiry.

Christine and Simon walked quietly down to the boathouse by the river. Without talking, they put the boat in the water, and sailed away across the river.

On the other side of the river they met two friends, Peter and Susan. Their friends were wearing white clothes, with *Greenworld* written on them. Simon and Christine also put on white clothes. Then they all got into the boat and sailed upstream, towards the paint factory.

It was a windy morning, and the waves on the river were quite big. But Christine was a good sailor, and in about half an hour, they reached the factory. Two photographers stood by the river, taking photos of them.

'OK, Simon, where is it?' shouted Christine.

'Over there, look – in front of that post!' he said. Christine sailed the boat towards the post. When they were near it, they could see under the water. It was the pipe that took the waste products out of the factory.

'OK, here!' shouted Simon. Christine turned the boat towards the wind, and Susan caught hold of the post. Then Simon and Peter climbed out of the boat into the water.

They put the boat in the water, and sailed away across the river.

The water was moving fast here, and they had to hold onto the pipe and the boat. Peter then took several strong paper bags out of the boat. The bags were small but very heavy, because they were filled with building cement. Peter passed the bags one at a time to Simon, and Simon went down under the water and pushed each bag into the pipe. A few minutes later the mouth of the pipe was full of bags of cement.

Simon came up out of the water for the last time. 'It's OK!' he shouted. 'We've done it! The cement is wet already, and in a few hours it'll be as hard as a rock. Nothing can come out of that pipe now!' The two men climbed back into the boat and smiled at the photographers. Then Simon stood up in the boat with Christine, and held up a long white sheet. On the sheet was written:

GREEN
WORLD
This pipe kills seals!

At that moment two things happened. A man ran out of the factory, shouting angrily. And the wind suddenly became stronger. It caught the sail and sent it quickly from one side of the boat to the other. The back of the sail hit Christine hard on the back of the head. She fell into the water, like a bag of potatoes. Then the wind caught the sail again and threw it back across the boat. This time the boat fell over on its side and lay with its sail under the water.

Simon was under the sail. The sail and the sheet were all around him, and for several seconds he could see nothing. Then he came up, into the air. He saw a foot

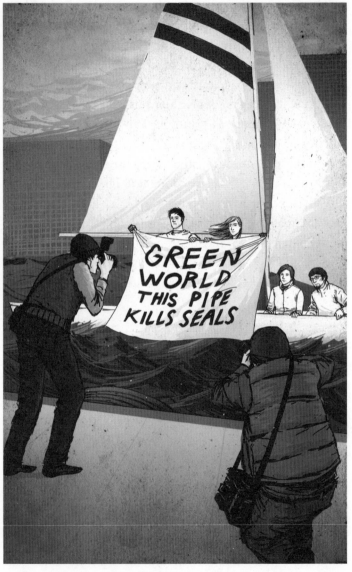

Simon and Christine held up a long white sheet.

kicking hard in the water beside him. Someone was moving under the sail. Quickly, he went down under the water again, and tried to help Peter. But Peter caught hold of Simon, and pulled him under water too. There was a quick, frightening fight, and then Simon managed to pull them both up, into the air again. They held onto the side of the boat together, breathing deeply.

Simon saw Susan holding onto the back of the boat. Then he heard someone shouting. He looked behind him and saw the man from the factory. He was shouting and pointing downstream. But Simon had water in his ears, and at first he couldn't hear the words very well. Then he understood.

'Look!' the man said. 'The girl! She's drowning!'

Simon looked downstream, where the man was pointing. He saw something white, floating, far away. It was not doing anything, just floating round and round, like a bag of old clothes on the water. Christine! The river was taking her quickly downstream, towards the sea.

Hurriedly, Simon began to swim after her. He was a good swimmer, but the white clothes slowed him down. He swam as fast as he could, but he seemed to go slowly, so slowly. The water seemed heavy, and held him back. For the rest of his life he would dream about that long, slow swim, towards a white body that floated quickly away in front of him.

At last he reached Christine. She was floating with her face down, unconscious. He tried to turn her over, but it was so difficult. She was heavy, and her arms fell back in the water when he dropped them. He got her face out of the water but her head fell backwards, lifeless, and she was not breathing. He caught hold of her face then, put his mouth over hers, and blew into it. He rested, and then blew into her mouth again, and again. Nothing happened.

He looked around him. They were in the middle of the river, moving quickly downstream. Here, it was about twenty-five metres to the bank, but about two hundred metres downstream a second river came in from the left. The bank was further away there, and the water moved faster. Simon was tired, and afraid. It had rained last night, and there was a lot of water moving downstream to the sea. The strong wind blew little waves into his face.

He began to swim on his back, pulling Christine towards the trees on the bank. He swam for half a minute, then stopped, and blew four times into her mouth. Once, he thought he saw her breathe, but he couldn't be sure. Her face was very white, and he had no idea if her heart was beating. The river was taking them quickly to the sea.

He swam harder, kicking strongly with his legs. Nearer – only five metres to go now. But the bank was moving past very quickly. There was a tree near the bank. Its branches were low over the water. Simon kicked hard, caught the branch, and held onto it. The water tried to pull him away. He took a deep breath, and blew strongly into Christine's mouth again. And this time, he was sure, she took a breath by herself, afterwards.

It took him nearly five minutes to pull her on to the bank. When they got there, he put her on the ground, breathed into her mouth again, and then felt for her heart.

Only five metres to go now.

At first he couldn't find it – his hands were too cold. Then – yes! – it was beating.

For another five minutes he helped her breathe, until he was sure she could do it by herself. Then he began to shiver. The wind made his wet clothes cold on his body. He wondered what to do. Then he looked down, and saw that Christine's eyes were open.

'Chris,' he said. 'Are you all right?'

She said something, but very quietly and he could not hear it. He lay down, and put his arms around her, to keep her warm. He could feel her heart beating, and her body breathing under him. Simon began to cry.

11

The Public Enquiry

Two days later, the Enquiry began. Scientists came from London to ask questions about the disease that was killing the seals. Before he had gone to Scotland, John had been to see David Wilson about the Enquiry. David Wilson had asked John to speak for the company.

'You're our chief biologist, John,' he said. 'You're an important man. They'll believe you.'

John said nothing. He didn't want to speak at the Enquiry, but he knew he had to. David Wilson smiled. Or at least, his mouth smiled. But his eyes watched John carefully, all the time, like the cold eyes of a fish.

'Think carefully about what you say, John. If you say the wrong thing next week, hundreds of people will lose their jobs. And the first person to lose his job will be you, John. I promise you that.'

The Enquiry room was crowded. There were a lot of journalists and photographers there, and a lot of people from the town and the factory too. John's train was late, and he caught a taxi from the station. When he came into the room, he saw Simon, sitting with the journalists. Christine was near him, with Andrew and some young people from Greenworld. John smiled at her, but she didn't smile back. She looks very white and ill, he thought. It's probably the baby. He remembered how ill his wife Rachel had been in the mornings, before Christine was born, and he smiled sadly to himself.

'Mr John Duncan, please!'

He walked to the front of the room. As he sat down, he saw David Wilson's cold, grey eyes watching him from the other side of the room. That man should be up here instead, he thought. He should tell his own lies.

A lawyer began to ask him questions. At first it was easy. John explained how long he had worked for the company, and how much paint the factory produced. Then the lawyer asked about the waste products.

'These are very dangerous chemicals, aren't they?' the lawyer said.

'Well yes, of course,' John answered. 'Most chemicals are dangerous if people aren't careful with them. But we're very careful with them in our factory. Everyone wears special clothing. We haven't had a single serious accident in three years.'

'I'm pleased to hear it,' said the lawyer. 'But what happens outside the factory? Do you really put these very dangerous chemicals into the river?'

'Yes, we do,' said John. There was a noise in the room. Someone near Christine shouted something angrily, and a policewoman told him to be quiet. John went on. 'Of course we put these chemicals in the river, but we don't put a lot in. Only two or three hundred litres every day. That's not much. And we check the river all the time – three times every day. There are usually only two parts per million, or less, in the water near the factory, and there is much less downstream. That's not dangerous.'

'Not dangerous, Mr Duncan?' said the lawyer slowly. 'Are you sure?'

'Yes, I am,' John said. He looked up, at the hundreds of eyes watching him. David Wilson's eyes, Christine's eyes, Simon's.

'I understand', the lawyer said slowly, 'that there has been an experiment with some rats. Some mother rats were given these chemicals in their drinking water, and some of their babies were born without legs. Is that right, Mr Duncan?'

John looked at the lawyer for the first time. He was a small, uninteresting-looking man in grey clothes, with grey hair and a thin face. He looks like a rat himself, John thought. The man's eyes were small and bright, and for some strange reason he had a newspaper in his hand. John began to feel afraid of him.

'Yes,' he said. 'That's right. But rats are much smaller than people, and they were given nearly five parts per million in their drinking water for ten days. That's very different. No one drinks the river water. It goes straight out to sea.'

He looked at the lawyer, and waited for the question about the seals. But it didn't come. Instead, the lawyer said: 'So you won't be worried, Mr Duncan, if someone falls into the river by accident, and drinks a lot of river water. Your own daughter, for example. There's no danger in an accident like that – is that right?'

John looked at Christine across the room. How big her eyes look in that white face, he thought. It must be because of the baby.

'No,' he said. 'There's no danger at all.'

There was the sound of voices in the room. The lawyer smiled a small, rat-like smile. He held his newspaper out towards John.

'You've been away in Scotland, Mr Duncan,' he said. 'Have you seen this?'

As John read the newspaper, his hands began to shake, and he had to hold the side of the table. There was a picture of Christine, standing up in a boat near the factory, and another picture of her lying in an ambulance, with Simon beside her. The headline said:

BIOLOGIST'S DAUGHTER NEARLY DROWNS IN RIVER

There was a long silence. He tried to read the newspaper carefully, but there was something wrong with his eyes. And his head was full of pictures of

'*You've been away in Scotland, Mr Duncan. Have you seen this?*'

Christine in the river, drowning. And his wife, Rachel, drowning in the storm, long ago.

He shook his head quickly from side to side, then took his glasses off and cleaned them.

'No,' he said in a quiet voice. 'I haven't read this before.'

'It's all right, Mr Duncan,' said the lawyer softly. 'Your daughter is safe. Her husband saved her, and she hasn't lost her baby. But she did drink a lot of river water. It was near the factory, too. You're not worried about that, are you?'

The lawyer's bright eyes were staring at him, like a rat that has just seen its food. Behind him, David Wilson suddenly stood up.

'That is a terrible question!' he shouted into the silence. 'You can't ask a man questions like that! Of course he's worried about his daughter! You must stop this Enquiry at once!'

'Just a minute, Mr Wilson,' said the lawyer. 'Mr Duncan can go in a minute. He just has to answer one question. Are you worried, because your daughter has drunk so much river water, Mr Duncan? Are you worried about her baby?'

John Duncan stared at the lawyer with fear in his eyes. Suddenly he hated him. He picked up the newspaper and threw it into the little man's rat-like face. '*Yes*!' he shouted wildly. 'Yes! Yes! Yes! Of course I'm worried about the baby! Of course it's dangerous! Now let me go!'

He ran down the room, out of the door, into the street. A hundred staring eyes watched him go.

12

The future

Six months later, John Duncan was living in a small flat near the sea. He had lost his job, and had had to sell his expensive house. He couldn't afford the payments on it.

From a window in his flat, he could look at the sea. He sat and looked at the cold, grey sea for hours, every day.

Christine would have her baby soon. He had bought lots of baby clothes to give her. His bedroom was full of baby clothes – little pink coats and trousers for a girl, blue ones for a boy. There were little soft toys too – teddy bears and small animals with blue, empty eyes.

But he hadn't given any of these things to her, because she wouldn't talk to him. When he went to see her, she closed the door in his face; when he rang, she put the phone down; when he wrote, she sent the letters back unopened.

There were a lot of books and magazines in his bedroom, too. But he kept them under his bed. He read them sometimes at night, but he didn't like to see them during the day. They were about babies, and the diseases that babies could get, before they were born. There were some terrible things in the books, terrible pictures. He didn't like to think about them, but he couldn't stop. He thought about them all day, all the time.

Today, as he sat staring out of the window at the sea, he could not stop his hands shaking. Every morning he rang the hospital, to ask if his daughter Christine

*For two hours John had sat by the telephone,
afraid to ring the hospital again.*

MacDonald was there. He had rung this morning, and a nurse had said yes, Christine was there, and the baby was coming. That had been four hours ago. For two hours John had sat by the telephone, afraid to ring the hospital again. Three times he had picked it up, and three times he had put it down again.

He picked it up again, and rang the number. Seven . . . five . . . eight . . . three . . . it was no good. He put the phone down again. He could not hear the news from the cold voice of a nurse over the telephone. He had to see the baby for himself.

He got up, put on his coat, and went downstairs. There was a cold wind outside, blowing from the sea. The sea and the sky were grey and miserable. He went into a shop and bought some flowers. He chose them carefully – bright red and yellow colours – and the shopkeeper put paper around them to keep them safe. John took them and walked quickly, nervously, along the windy road by the sea, towards the hospital.

It was raining out at sea. Already the rain was falling on the sandbanks where the seals used to live. Soon it would be falling on the town. John Duncan shivered, and turned his coat collar up. Then, with his bright flowers in his hand, he walked on, into the winter wind.

GLOSSARY

acid *(n)* a chemical liquid that burns

afford to have enough money for something

article a report in a newspaper

bank (of a river) the ground along the side of a river

biologist a scientist who studies animals and plants

breathe to take air in and send it out through the nose and
mouth

cement grey powder that becomes hard like rock when mixed
with water

chemical *(n)* something solid or liquid used in chemistry

chemist a scientist who studies chemistry

collar the piece of a shirt or coat that goes round the neck

comfort *(v)* to try to make someone feel happier

congratulations a word said to someone who has been lucky or
done well

develop to change something and make it bigger or better

dilute to make a liquid thinner or not so strong by adding
water

downstream in the direction in which a river moves (towards
the sea)

drown to die in water because you cannot breathe

environment all the natural things around us (land, air, water,
plants, etc.)

experiment *(n)* a test on something to find out what happens
and to learn something new

float to stay on top of the water

future the days, years, etc. that will come after today

government the group of people who control a country

Heaven's sake (for . . .) words people say to show they are
angry or surprised

journalist a person who writes for newspapers, television or radio

kick *(v)* to move a foot very quickly and suddenly

kiss *(v)* to touch someone with your lips in a loving way

lawyer someone whose job is helping people with the law

liar a person who says things that are not true

local belonging to one place or area

magnifying glass a special glass that makes small things look bigger

nasty bad, not nice

nervous afraid, worried

paint *(n)* a coloured liquid used to change the colour of other things

part per million how much something is diluted by, e.g. 2 litres of waste products in each million litres of river water = two parts per million

point *(v)* to show with your finger or hand where something is

produce *(v)* to make something

proud feeling pleased about something you have or did

Public Enquiry a special meeting when people can ask questions or argue about the plans or actions of a company, the government, etc.

rat a small grey or brown animal with a long tail

result *(n)* what happens because of something (e.g. an experiment)

sample *(n)* a small piece of something, which is an example of the rest

sandbank a large area of sand in a river or the sea

scientist someone who studies science (the study of natural things)

seal *(n)* an animal that lives both in the sea and on land

sewage works a place where sewage (human waste) is cleaned before it goes into the sea or a river

shiver   to shake because you are cold or frightened

skiing   a sport when people move over snow on skis (long pieces of wood)

son-in-law   the husband of your daughter

spill (past tense **spilt**)   to make a liquid run or fall out of a container by mistake

teddy bear   a furry animal which is a popular child's toy

test *(v)*   to look at something carefully to find out how good it is

thoughtful   thinking

toy   something for a child to play with

unconscious   a kind of sleep, when a person is ill or hurt

upstream   up the river away from the sea (the opposite of downstream)

waste products   something that is made (but which is useless and not needed) during the making of something else

wave *(n)*   a movement of water in the sea or a river

ACTIVITIES

Before Reading

1 Read the back cover, and the introduction on the first page. What kind of person do you think John Duncan is going to be? Choose Y (Yes) or N (No) for each of these ideas.

1 He is a murderer. Y/N

2 He is an honest man who makes a big mistake. Y/N

3 He is a man who likes money. Y/N

4 He is a man who needs money. Y/N

5 He is a man who loves his children. Y/N

6 He is a dishonest man. Y/N

2 What do you think will happen in the story? Choose the words you prefer to complete these sentences.

1 John Duncan *tells* / *doesn't tell* the truth about his job.

2 The chemical factory kills some *people* / *animals*.

3 John Duncan *loses* / *leaves* his job at the chemical factory.

4 By the end of the story John Duncan is a *rich* / *poor* man.

3 The story introduction talks about different kinds of crime. Which of these crimes do you think is worse? Why?

1 A man who kills his wife's lover.

2 A drunk driver who kills somebody in a car accident.

3 Someone who knows the name of a murderer, but doesn't tell the police.

ACTIVITIES

While Reading

Read Chapters 1 and 2. Choose the best question-word for these questions, and then answer them.

What / How / Why

1 . . . old was John Duncan?
2 . . . were John Duncan's two interests in life?
3 . . . did John Duncan stop working as a biologist?
4 . . . happened to John Duncan's wife?
5 . . . did the paint factory need a biologist?
6 . . . did John Duncan feel about David Wilson?
7 . . . long had John Duncan been without a job?
8 . . . had Christine Duncan never been skiing?

Read Chapters 3 and 4. Here are some untrue sentences about them. Change them into true sentences.

1 The company had not brought any new jobs to the town.
2 The waste products from the factory went into the sea.
3 The factory was five kilometres from the sea.
4 The town's drinking water came from the river at the river mouth.
5 John had spilt some of the waste products on his leg, and was very worried about it.
6 John bought a computer for his children.
7 When Mary came to dinner, the evening went well.
8 Nobody enjoyed watching the seals on the sandbank.

Read Chapters 5 and 6. Use these words from the story to complete John Duncan's report.

before, born, chemicals, diluted, drinking, experiments, eyes, legs, less, machines, million, no, parts, per, produced, rats, results, safe, test, waste, were, without

Several _____ were done on rats to _____ the waste products which are _____ by the factory. These chemicals are _____ and on most days _____ than two parts per _____ go into the river. Two groups of mother _____ were given _____ water which contained the _____ products: the first group had five _____ per million; the second group had two parts _____ million. When the baby rats were _____, in the first group some had no _____, some had _____ ears, and some had six _____. In the second group some _____ born _____ legs.

These _____ show that it is not _____ to put these _____ in the river. The company must build _____ to clean up the waste products _____ they leave the factory.

Before you read Chapter 7, can you guess what happens next? Choose Y (Yes) or N (No) for each sentence.

1 John leaves the paint factory. Y/N
2 The company builds the new machines. Y/N
3 John tells the newspapers about the chemicals. Y/N
4 The factory closes and everybody loses their jobs. Y/N
5 Animals and fish in the river begin to die. Y/N
6 The chemicals get into the town's drinking water. Y/N
7 Your own idea.

Read Chapters 7 to 10, and then match these halves of sentences.

1 when he told her that the river water was not dangerous.
2 Christine was unconscious when she fell in the river . . .
3 Although John didn't want Christine to marry Simon, . . .
4 but she was pleased that he hadn't asked her to marry him.
5 in order to stop the chemicals going into the river.
6 Christine did not believe her father . . .
7 so she nearly drowned before Simon saved her.
8 in the end he agreed to the marriage.
9 The Greenworld people put bags of cement in the pipe . . .
10 Mary liked John and felt sorry for him, . . .

Before you read Chapter 11, can you guess the answers to these questions?

1 Will John be angry with Christine, or worried about her?
2 What will happen to Christine's baby?
3 What will John do at the Enquiry?

Read Chapters 11 and 12, and then answer these questions.

1 Why did John have to speak at the Enquiry?
2 Why didn't John know about Christine's accident?
3 What did the lawyer show John at the Enquiry?
4 Why did John lose his job?
5 Why hadn't John given the toys and clothes to Christine?
6 Why was John afraid for Christine?

ACTIVITIES

After Reading

1 Complete this newspaper story about Christine's accident. (Use as many words as you like.)

BIOLOGIST'S DAUGHTER NEARLY

DROWNS IN RIVER

Yesterday a young woman nearly _____ when she was sailing with _____ near the _____. Christine MacDonald, aged 18, was hit _____ by a sail and was _____ when she _____. Her body began to _____, but _____ shouted a warning, and her husband, Simon MacDonald, swam after her and _____.

Mrs MacDonald is the daughter of John Duncan, who is _____. His daughter Christine belongs to Greenworld, an _____ which believes that chemicals _____ are killing _____. She and her friends put _____ into the factory's waste pipe to stop _____.

Mrs Macdonald is going to _____ and doctors are very worried because she _____ from _____.

2 Do you think John Duncan was a good father, or not? Make a list of the good things that he did for his children, and the bad things.

He was a good father because . . .
He was a bad father because . . .

3 Here is a conversation between David Wilson and Mary Carter. The conversation is in the wrong order. Write it out in the correct order and put in the speakers' names. Wilson speaks first (number 6).

1 _____ 'The seals do. And look at *their* babies.'

2 _____ 'Yes, they are. Look at those baby rats!'

3 _____ 'I've come to tell you that I'm leaving, David.'

4 _____ 'OK, so you care. But what can *I* do about it?'

5 _____ 'You know why. Because of the waste products that are going into the river.'

6 _____ 'Hello, Mary, what can I do for you?'

7 _____ 'Oh, them! Mary, I've told you, those chemicals aren't dangerous!'

8 _____ 'Seals! Who cares about a few seals?'

9 _____ 'But they're rats, Mary, not people. And nobody drinks water from the river mouth. You know that!'

10 _____ 'You can buy machines to take out some of the chemicals before the waste products go into the river.'

11 _____ 'So the seals have to die because you can't afford the machines?'

12 _____ 'Leaving? But why?'

13 _____ 'No, I can't, Mary. The company can't afford them.'

14 _____ 'Well, you don't have to worry about *my* job any more, David. I'm leaving tomorrow. Goodbye.'

15 _____ 'I care. I care about everything in the river.'

16 _____ 'Yes. People come first, Mary. Four hundred people work here. That's what I worry about – their jobs!'

4 **Here is David Wilson's letter to the newspaper. Use the linking words below to complete it.**

although / and / and / because / but / if / since / so / that / where / which / why

Sir: your article yesterday about our factory contained some information _____ was completely untrue, _____ I wonder _____ your journalist got his facts from. Scientists do not yet know _____ the seals are dying. _____ our factory puts some waste products into the river, it is less than two parts per million, _____ a lot more waste comes from the sewage works. It is also untrue to say _____ the river water is unsafe for people. All the town's drinking water comes from five kilometres upstream, _____ nobody can drink water which contains our waste products.

   Our company cares about this town _____ a lot of our workers live here. We have created four hundred new jobs _____ we came here ten years ago. We can clean up the waste _____ we spend two million pounds on machines to do it, _____ that would mean fewer jobs for the people of this town.
David Wilson,
Managing Director, Wiltech Paints

5 **Who is right in this story – David Wilson, or Greenworld? Do you agree (A) or disagree (D) with the ideas below? Think of some more ideas of your own.**

Greenworld is right, because . . .
1 All rivers should be free from dangerous chemicals.

2 There is always a chance that people will drink the water by accident.

3 Animals need clean water as well as people.

David Wilson is right, because . . .

1 No chemicals go into the town's drinking water.

2 Jobs for people are more important than seals dying.

3 The river water is already dirty because of the sewage.

6 **What was John Duncan thinking at these moments in his life? Complete the sentences in your own words.**

1 If I get this job at the paint factory, _____

2 If Mary likes my children, perhaps _____

3 If the baby rats are born healthy, _____

4 If Wilson agrees to build the machines, _____

5 If I leave this job, _____

6 If I stay here and say nothing, _____

7 It was a terrible mistake to _____

7 **What happens next? Choose some of these ideas and write a new ending of your own for the story.**

- Christine's baby is born healthy / dead / without legs.
- Christine is pleased to see her father / is angry with him for a while / never speaks to him again.
- Christine and Simon stay in the town / go to another country / have more children / have no more children.
- The factory cleans up the river / does nothing.
- John Duncan gets a new job / never works again / joins Greenworld / finds a kind woman to marry him.

ABOUT THE AUTHOR

Tim Vicary is an experienced teacher and writer, and has written several stories for the Oxford Bookworms Library. Many of these are in the Thriller & Adventure series, such as *Skyjack!* (at Stage 3), or in the True Stories series, such as *The Brontë Story* (also at Stage 3), which is about the lives of the famous novelists, Charlotte, Emily, and Anne Brontë.

Tim Vicary has two children, and keeps dogs, cats, and horses. He lives and works in York, in the north of England, and has also published two long novels, *The Blood upon the Rose* and *Cat and Mouse*.

OXFORD BOOKWORMS LIBRARY

Classics • Crime & Mystery • Factfiles • Fantasy & Horror
Human Interest • Playscripts • Thriller & Adventure
True Stories • World Stories

The OXFORD BOOKWORMS LIBRARY provides enjoyable reading in English, with a wide range of classic and modern fiction, non-fiction, and plays. It includes original and adapted texts in seven carefully graded language stages, which take learners from beginner to advanced level. An overview is given on the next pages.

All Stage 1 titles are available as audio recordings, as well as over eighty other titles from Starter to Stage 6. All Starters and many titles at Stages 1 to 4 are specially recommended for younger learners. Every Bookworm is illustrated, and Starters and Factfiles have full-colour illustrations.

The OXFORD BOOKWORMS LIBRARY also offers extensive support. Each book contains an introduction to the story, notes about the author, a glossary, and activities. Additional resources include tests and worksheets, and answers for these and for the activities in the books. There is advice on running a class library, using audio recordings, and the many ways of using Oxford Bookworms in reading programmes. Resource materials are available on the website <www.oup.com/bookworms>.

The *Oxford Bookworms Collection* is a series for advanced learners. It consists of volumes of short stories by well-known authors, both classic and modern. Texts are not abridged or adapted in any way, but carefully selected to be accessible to the advanced student.

You can find details and a full list of titles in the *Oxford Bookworms Library Catalogue* and *Oxford English Language Teaching Catalogues*, and on the website <www.oup.com/bookworms>.

THE OXFORD BOOKWORMS LIBRARY
GRADING AND SAMPLE EXTRACTS

STARTER • 250 HEADWORDS

present simple – present continuous – imperative –
can/cannot, must – going to (future) – simple gerunds …

Her phone is ringing – but where is it?

Sally gets out of bed and looks in her bag. No phone. She looks under the bed. No phone. Then she looks behind the door. There is her phone. Sally picks up her phone and answers it. ***Sally's Phone***

STAGE 1 • 400 HEADWORDS

… past simple – coordination with *and*, *but*, *or* –
subordination with *before, after, when, because, so* …

I knew him in Persia. He was a famous builder and I worked with him there. For a time I was his friend, but not for long. When he came to Paris, I came after him – I wanted to watch him. He was a very clever, very dangerous man. ***The Phantom of the Opera***

STAGE 2 • 700 HEADWORDS

… present perfect – *will* (future) – *(don't) have to, must not, could* –
comparison of adjectives – simple *if* clauses – past continuous –
tag questions – *ask/tell* + infinitive …

While I was writing these words in my diary, I decided what to do. I must try to escape. I shall try to get down the wall outside. The window is high above the ground, but I have to try. I shall take some of the gold with me – if I escape, perhaps it will be helpful later. ***Dracula***

STAGE 3 • 1000 HEADWORDS

... should, may – present perfect continuous – *used to* – past perfect –
causative – relative clauses – indirect statements ...

Of course, it was most important that no one should see
Colin, Mary, or Dickon entering the secret garden. So Colin
gave orders to the gardeners that they must all keep away
from that part of the garden in future. *The Secret Garden*

STAGE 4 • 1400 HEADWORDS

... past perfect continuous – passive (simple forms) –
would conditional clauses – indirect questions –
relatives with *where/when* – gerunds after prepositions/phrases ...

I was glad. Now Hyde could not show his face to the world
again. If he did, every honest man in London would be proud
to report him to the police. *Dr Jekyll and Mr Hyde*

STAGE 5 • 1800 HEADWORDS

... future continuous – future perfect –
passive (modals, continuous forms) –
would have conditional clauses – modals + perfect infinitive ...

If he had spoken Estella's name, I would have hit him. I was so
angry with him, and so depressed about my future, that I could
not eat the breakfast. Instead I went straight to the old house.
Great Expectations

STAGE 6 • 2500 HEADWORDS

... passive (infinitives, gerunds) – advanced modal meanings –
clauses of concession, condition

When I stepped up to the piano, I was confident. It was as if I
knew that the prodigy side of me really did exist. And when I
started to play, I was so caught up in how lovely I looked that
I didn't worry how I would sound. *The Joy Luck Club*

BOOKWORMS • THRILLER & ADVENTURE • STAGE 3

Skyjack!

TIM VICARY

When a large plane is hijacked, the Prime Minister looks at the list of passengers and suddenly becomes very, very frightened.

There is a name on the list that the Prime Minister knows very well – too well. There is someone on that plane who will soon be dead – if the hijackers can find out who he is!

And there isn't much time. One man lies dead on the runway. In a few minutes the hijackers will use their guns again. And the Prime Minister knows who they are going to kill.

BOOKWORMS • CRIME & MYSTERY • STAGE 3

As the Inspector Said and Other Stories

RETOLD BY JOHN ESCOTT

The murder plan seems so neat, so clever. How can it possibly fail? And when Sonia's stupid, boring little husband is dead, she will be free to marry her handsome lover. But perhaps the boring little husband is not so stupid after all . . .

Murder plans that go wrong, a burglar who makes a bad mistake, a famous jewel thief who meets a very unusual detective . . . These five stories from the golden age of crime writing are full of mystery and surprises.